T0169945

DRAGAN DRAGOJLOVIĆ

DEATH'S HOMELAND

Translated by:
Stanislava Lazarević

Curbstone Press

A Lannan Translation Selection
with Special Thanks to Patrick Lannan and
the Lannan Foundation Board of Directors

Connecticut Commission
on Culture & Tourism

This book was published with the support of the
Connecticut Commission on Culture and
Tourism, the Connecticut State Legislature
through the Office of Policy and Management,
the Lannan Foundation, and donations from
many individuals. We are very grateful for this support.

Library of Congress Cataloging-in-Publication Data

Dragojlovic, Dragan, 1941-
[Zavicaj smrti. English]
  Death's homeland / Dragan Dragojlovic ; translated by
Stanislava Lazarevic.
    p. cm.
  ISBN 978-1-931896-45-0 (pbk. : alk. paper)
  1. Yugoslav War, 1991-1995—Poetry. I. Lazarevic, Stanislava.
II. Title.

  PG1419.14.R25Z2413 2008
  891.8'215—dc22

                                        2008008284

CURBSTONE PRESS   321 Jackson Street   Willimantic, CT 06226
phone: 860-423-5110   e-mail: info@curbstone.org
www.curbstone.org

CONTENTS

STONE OF WOE

Stone of woe / 1

There is no one left / 2

Before the unchangeable / 3

Early snow on the mountains / 4

The blind guide / 5

What befell us / 6

Under death's wing / 7

Soot and ruins / 8

The landscape of dawn / 9

Merciless daybreak / 10

Sins may have been expiated / 11

FRUIT OF HELL

Fruit of hell / 15

The living and the dead / 16

Confirmed news / 17

A painter's monologue / 18

The day will be over / 19

The sun above a naked forest / 20

The space of infinity / 21

Ruins / 22

I know what Hell is / 23

In spite of everything / 24

Let the war be damned / 25

Magnificent emptiness / 26

War talk / 27

Words instead of forgiveness / 28

CREEPING IN OF EVIL
Vienna and Deutschland / 31
Servants of their own hatred / 32
Earth's bitter bread / 33
Is this me? / 34
The secret of death / 35
God's love / 36
Lords of evil / 37
God Interest / 38

WARRIORS
In the waste wind / 41
Dead warriors / 42
Trenches / 43
In the underground shelter / 44
A brief announcement / 45
Ready for death / 46
Celestial warriors / 47
Winter's might / 48
The earth will turn into desert / 49
Only one star / 50
Before death / 51

THE REALM OF THE DEAD
The realm of the dead / 55
Dreams from another time / 56
Wormwood and rosemary / 57
Gifts / 58
Kingdom of the dead / 59
The message / 60
The secret / 61

I will cry in Heaven / 62

Posthumous flute / 63

Across the moonlit garden / 64

An unfamiliar dead man / 65

GLORY ETERNAL

Glory eternal / 69

STONE OF WOE

STONE OF WOE

However deep
this pain may have sunk into the heart,
the next one will sink deeper;
however loud this shriek may have sounded,
the next one will be softer,
filling the wasteland
from a strange inner voice.

Console yourself.
We shall be a stone
hardened by grief,
a stone of woe,
a stone that can dwell
neither in hope, nor in memories,
a stone block doomed
to become a ruin.

THERE IS NO ONE LEFT

Hot July sweeps in
through the door of a ravaged house,
lighting fireflies like icon lamps
over the empty silence
where the songs of harvesters
enter from somewhere,
trembling like cobwebs
in the night breeze
descending from the Milky Way –
here, where
but for our former life
and present death –
there is no one left.

BEFORE THE UNCHANGEABLE

So many vain wishes,
so much of the possible
that has become impossible
surrounds me
on this frosty day.
I can't suppress my suffering
before the unchangeable.

The only mercy
is the sun,
this good, old sun
that gives me warmth.

EARLY SNOW ON THE MOUNTAINS

Bleeding dawn, the stopped day.
On the horizon,
a peculiar reluctance
of sun to rise.
Unripe blackberries
seem sweeter
than communion wine.
The darkness of the returning night
stands victoriously on my palm.
Did I dream in vain?
I ask, as I look at
early snow on the mountains.

THE BLIND GUIDE

It may have been right
for my tireless hope
that had guided me so blindly
to look at itself
the way I am looking at death,
at everyday death,
driving war chariots
across the regions
where my dreams grew up.

WHAT BEFELL US

Youth has vanished.
And a generation.
And towns where our
hope grew.

What befell us
no one can tell.
All that is left is
your grave.
   The only place I have
   to come to,

my darling,
so I can cry.

UNDER DEATH'S WING

Under death's wing
night has moved into the sky.
Patches of fog
flutter above the valleys.

No one's here.
Silence paces
along morning's trail.
The wind reaches for
the distance in vain
to find the voice
that was extinguished.

.

SOOT AND RUINS

In the village
there were no houses,
or stables, or fences,
only soot and ruins.
And the dead, decaying
in the sluggish winter sun.

When our count was completed,
a flock of wild shadows
screeched above our
heads.
Already the bitterness of dusk
blanketed everything.

We didn't know what to do.
But when someone lit a candle
we were dumbfounded:
from the other side of reality
the dead were staring at us
in surprise,
as if we had never existed.

THE LANDSCAPE OF DAWN

The familiar landscape of dawn
seems to be emerging from
somnolent oblivion.
The smell of burning
is still spreading
bitter smoke over a bitter world.

A fragment of the moon
hangs over the shredded forest,
already the sun is rising.
The soul chokes and shrinks.
I long to celebrate
what God commenced
on some remote day,
but within rifle range
the shooting begins again.

MERCILESS DAYBREAK

Merciless daybreak
reveals the doings of the night.
Sunbeams shed their warmth
on the dead in vain.
Death is indifferent,
like eternity.
The barking of dogs
through the deserted woods
is lost in the wind
and among the leaves.
The heart goes on counting
the rosary of the stars
that have betrayed us.

SINS MAY HAVE BEEN EXPIATED

My sins may have been expiated.
And my speechlessness stings more
than my poem.
And this silence is louder
than the marching army,
than the cries of mothers.

My sins may have been expiated.
Maybe I'm not guilty at all
of coming into this world.
But even so, even now,
I still can't find God's gate.
My gate is already open.
I have fled from myself
and wander hopelessly,
without a signpost.

FRUIT OF HELL

FRUIT OF HELL

Standing beneath the midday sky
beyond which the horizon expands
into emptiness,
he is trying to imagine
what the landscape of his childhood
looks like,
through which so much blood is flowing.

He tries to touch the distance
the rumble
of the denuded hills.

There, beyond that rumble,
mortars shake the sky,
shedding fruit of Hell,
a flaming torrent
that extinguishes everything.

THE LIVING AND THE DEAD

What a procession:
coffins in a long line,
shrouded in heaven
and tears,
facing eternity
which awaits them
in their collective tomb.

What a procession
by the oak trees
that rustle gently
in whose spreading branches
the day and the birds are soothed,

and the landscape between
earth and sky is
choked by wailing.

CONFIRMED NEWS

There where
we once lived so happily
war and chaos
have proclaimed
their kingdom.

And death,
master of oblivion,
spreads castles under the earth
because there is
nothing left above it.

A PAINTER'S MONOLOGUE

Jailer of a bloody sunrise,
graveyard warden, builder of a tower
the foundations of which
have been crushed,
or someone else
but not the one who used to be
while he shaped with colors
the naïve spaces of his soul,
his empty soul
that can only wonder: God,
why could it not have been different?

THE DAY WILL BE OVER

The day will pass like this
and so will the night.
The mortars will strike tomorrow
just as they did today.

We have become accustomed
to dying, and being wounded,
but what are we to do
with so much grief?

THE SUN ABOVE A NAKED FOREST

Such grace
on this January day!
Such a gift from Heaven!
Through the fog
through smoke and shooting,
through the frost
that makes fingers stick to metal,
the sun has emerged,
a magnificent sun
above the naked forest.

Only a single ray breaks
through this unexpected silence,
only a single step of the year –
the forest will put out new leaves
to hide this death,

to erase all trace of it
from the face of the earth.

THE SPACE OF INFINITY

I used to be a man
who played with his hopes
at night,
hiding behind his dreams
during the day.

The limits were around me,
infinity was within.

Now I am silent so I cannot witness
how every gunshot,
each new death,
constricts the space of my infinity,

chasing me into a kennel,
as the void grows
bigger and bigger.

RUINS

This was once a church,
this was the altar,
the frescoes, the icons.
Now the scorched colors
pray to the god of fire
from the ashes.

Saints and angels
are voiceless
in this temple of God
which has no walls
and is roofless,
which looks at its reflection
in the sky
and is silent.

I KNOW WHAT HELL IS

I have known the fire of lead
and the earth ablaze.
I can say:
I know what hell is.

Now, I gather emptiness.
Unfamiliar sounds
fall upon my heart
like tumbling rocks.

Sleep would be welcome
to shorten this night,
to bring daylight
to the doorstep
where the powers of darkness
seduce and bring to naught
life and memory.

IN SPITE OF EVERYTHING

The days of life
have been spent.
Emptiness spreads
over the earth
and resembles death.

In spite of everything,
music is heard
from somewhere,
the skies seem
to be clearing
over this wasteland
as if, suddenly,
the world
has been transformed.

LET THE WAR BE DAMNED

Let the war be damned,
and the hell where
the armies of death
hide my homeland,
where wild winds
of revenge
stir wild blood.
Damned be what goodness
cannot redress,
the word and the mouth
from which emerges hatred
instead of love.
Let them be damned, oh earth,
those surveyors of death
here, where God only
sets the final boundaries –
and Time, his sole
executor.

MAGNIFICENT EMPTINESS

What sorrow mounts,
what emptiness,
a void instead of a heart
in our breasts!

As if the time
when we were happy
had flown into the sky
taking away our happiness,
In the pathless distances
it seeks a new home.

What anxiety,
what magnificent emptiness
throbs inside us!

WAR TALK

It is no good talking of war,
of disaster.
A few words will do:
he was dear to you,
you cherished with reverence
the breadth of his soul.

All you have to do
is forget.

WORDS INSTEAD OF FORGIVENESS

It makes so little sense
to keep silent, or to talk.

The days are short,
deaths linger on.
Towers made of ash
were home to no one.

The days are short,
grief lingers.
When I kneel to pray,
hope, have pity on me.

It makes so little sense
to talk,
and words of forgiveness
uttered before a man
are also uttered before God.

CREEPING IN OF EVIL

VIENNA AND DEUTSCHLAND

Princip's shots
seem to be heard.*

And History gasps, confused,
pressing her heart,
asking random passersby
which path to take.
There is great clamor
which is heard: Forward into the past!
Amid the tumult, in the dust,
a black-and-yellow fox
with a huge, blood-stained tail
is getting its feet
tangled up.
The ignorant wonder
what are the stakes
of Deutschland, and imperial
Vienna, in the Balkan death dance,
here, where they have so often
built vast cemeteries.

*In 1914, Gavrilo Princip assassinated Austro-Hungarian Archduke Franc
Ferdinand in Sarajevo. That served as a pretext for Austria-Hungary to declare
war upon Serbia which in turn triggered World War I.

SERVANTS OF THEIR OWN HATRED

Servants of their own hatred
and death,
what can they produce,
laden with so many graves
here on earth,
where everything is longer
than human life?

EARTH'S BITTER BREAD

Dark deep valleys,
deeply cleft gorges
intersect the human heart,
digging trenches
from which brothers
shoot at each other
under the star of death,
behind the bitter bread of earth.

Let no one tell me
that our aspirations
and our hope
can make this world better.

How sweet would it be
to dream at the source of the tear
that without fail defeats us.

IS THIS ME?

Is this myself now
or what I used to be
or the future, deserted,
slipping into my clothes
and leaving
on a train that roars
through my mind
like tanks crossing a field?

Is this myself
or my shadow
talking with me
while death is waiting
to head off somewhere

as I embark
on my blood-stained memory?

THE SECRET OF DEATH

The secret of death
abides within this body,
in this heart that remembers
the Creator's orders,
bridging the distance
between good and evil
in a single stroke.

The secret of death
is in the day,
in the hands of the clock
that turn the celestial wheel
along the path of the earth

on this ground
we die for,
which no one will even notice
once we are gone.

GOD'S LOVE

It is all here,
in these ruins,
in this scorched town
full of graves
and unburied bodies.

The day and the night
are here, too,
and the sun and the stars.
Here are the winds
and the rains,
the snows and the frosts,
even the moon playing
with its quarters and phases
above the battlefield

as if it were all here
except for God's love,
and God, the one they pray to.

LORDS OF EVIL

It's as if we'd never lived together,
as if we had arrived
from different worlds,

as if we were subjects of hatred,
the chosen lot of misery.

Can it be
that God gives to everyone
according to his nature,
or have we been betrayed
by fate,

or is it that the lords of evil
found blind executioners
in all of us?

GOD INTEREST

What is happening?
Where are we?
What time is it?
Look, the murderous hand is
drawing out old maps,
recasting the roles.
Mentioning history
and justice
doesn't make any sense
now

when merciless God Interest
is overshadowing
the world.

WARRIORS

IN THE WASTE WIND

Just let luck be with us
when we charge
across the bullets.
Let luck be with us
and mother's prayer
since we must tempt death.

Just let luck be with us
and the quiver
of a mother's soul
in the waste wind
that hums here
and above
amid merciless stars.

DEAD WARRIORS

Dead warriors
pace silently along.

When they come across
a token of the sun,
singing bursts out
to glorify light,
and for an instant
they seem to be ordinary,
living people.

Just for an instant,
until empty eternity
falls silent once again.

TRENCHES

Gunshots and explosions,
faithful servants of death,
don't allow us to raise
our heads
above the trenches,
from the mud
where life has concealed itself,
where spring, too,
has hidden away
fearing to set off
across meadows and woods,
into the realm of death.

IN THE UNDERGROUND SHELTER

We've been pulled back
from the front line to rest.
Between the logs
a star descends into the shelter.
I play with it instead of sleeping.
It is mellow and pale,
like memory.
When I close my eyes,
my dead comrades
begin to play with it.
The distance between dreams
and reality
vanishes in the thickness
of the night,
and the star that descended
from the sky
cannot climb back to its home.

A BRIEF ANNOUNCEMENT

A freezing morning.
Bare trees
loaded with moans.
Neither the wind,
nor daylight,
nothing promises hope.
The war is here to stay.

READY FOR DEATH

A warrior dies
as one who is ready
to die should.
He dies quickly,
not thinking of glory.

A warrior dies.
The pain, the bitterness,
even hope
matter no more.
He has fulfilled his duty.
His soul does not fear
ultimate death.

CELESTIAL WARRIORS

Some warriors are
in the star-strewn sky,
others are hidden
behind the clouds.

You can see them clearly
charging at one
another,
charging and falling.

The more attentive will
also hear shouting.
It echoes against
the deserted land.

WINTER'S MIGHT

A translucent sky,
blue in the midst of night,
full of frostbitten stars,
speaks of winter's might
which neither bullets,
nor even death
can evade.

THE EARTH WILL TURN INTO DESERT

I can see from here
that death is no loss
on an earth that will turn into
desert
when might
overpowers truth –
which not even God
thought about
when he created the world.

ONLY ONE STAR

Rain and darkness.
An occasional explosion
shatters the silence.
There is nothing
that could shed
light
in this darkness.
Just a patch of sky
that is clearing.

What joy
a single star
can bring!

BEFORE DEATH

Through the underbrush
and branches
we pace along a path
unmarked by signposts
seen in a dream
while patches of fog
flee across
narrow clearings.

Just let us remain strong,
let us preserve our spirit,
let not the bullets
stop us halfway through.

Let not death
forestall us
before we arrive
where we must.

THE REALM OF THE DEAD

THE REALM OF THE DEAD

He was wary of bullets,
pulling his cap over one eye,
as if he were sleeping.
The plateau was long
and all the broader
as the trail of his blood
reached farther
than daylight
the moment he opened
the door of eternity
and recognized
the realm of the dead.

DREAMS FROM ANOTHER TIME

Through ruins and flames
dreams from another time
are fleeting.
I lie on the side of the road,
winding up in the distance.
I revolve around myself,
around the sky
all alone,
a ruin amid ruins.

WORMWOOD AND ROSEMARY

Wormwood and rosemary
she will pick tonight
when she reaches
the gardens of heaven.

She will pick wormwood
and rosemary,
and unfamiliar flowers
for the wedding
that will not happen.

GIFTS

They brought offerings
before the crooked cross,
a towel instead of a wedding present,
apples instead of a ring,
flowers and tears.

They brought offerings,
his closest ones, to ease
his first night in death,

to hide away in their grief
all that was,
all that will never be.

KINGDOM OF THE DEAD

Silently
darkness descends
from the sky.
Unafraid of bullets
it lands on our pillows
for the night.

Stars carve
a void inside us,
as the victims' souls
sail away in a yellow boat
to the kingdom of the dead.

THE MESSAGE

Only in loss
do we see the truth.
However light-hearted
it all seemed,
how profoundly,
how boundlessly
I loved you,
I say now when
you cannot hear me,
when the bullets
are quicker than words
and life.

THE SECRET

His soul now paces
across the cloudy sky
which is sometimes
creased by lightning,
and roaring resounds
in the distance
like a thunder of cannons.

The sound of cannons
means nothing to him now.
Nor can thunders harm him
his consummate soul
which has now
grasped the secret
the body could not fathom.

The rain pouring down
over his grave
does not understand either.

I WILL CRY IN HEAVEN

The pain seems to abate.

What do I care for the sky,
for the wan moon,
for the fickle stars
that were visible
but a moment ago?

What do I care
for the morning
for the meadows where
I gathered the sorrow
of this day?

What do I care
for my dear ones?
Now that I have no strength,
I will cry in heaven,
What else is there
to fill eternity?

POSTHUMOUS FLUTE

Explosions of mortar shells
are an infernal necklace
around the neck of night.
Tender, as mother's grace,
is the occasional silence
observing its reflection
in the fires
that burn quietly in the distance.
In the void we call
heaven
someone plays
a posthumous flute.

ACROSS THE MOONLIT GARDEN

Across the moonlit garden
he runs towards the well.

He runs through shadows
of apple trees,
through the mellow scent
of wounded leaves.
The beating of drums
 is heard from afar.

 He runs without turning back.
His younger brother
has already fallen.
He runs. Barefoot, he treads
from one star to another.
The sky slowly descends
into the darkness
down a long marble path.

AN UNFAMILIAR DEAD MAN

Night thins out.
Day paces slowly
across the valleys
where our death
stopped for the evening.

We sprawl in low-lying
trenches.
Instead of birds,
invisible shots screech,
and an unfamiliar dead man,
fearlessly,
walks across the fields.

GLORY ETERNAL

GLORY ETERNAL

May glory eternal be with you
who fell
for Serbia,
may your wounds be blessed,
my brother in hope.

May all your delusions
be forgiven.
May your pain be eased
in heaven.
Forgive your murderer.
Pray for those
upon whom you have inflicted
suffering and death.

My brother in sin and misfortune,
do not criticize
my attempt to glorify
what transcends all words:
your sacrifice.

Choking with pain
to the point of screaming,
dare I wonder
whether it could have been different,
and whether history and hope
outlive our death.

I remain silent
repeating to myself:
you did what you could,
let God complete the rest.

DRAGAN DRAGOJLOVIĆ was born in 1941 in Serbia. After receiving his M.A. in Economics at Belgrade University, he worked in economic planning and served in government positions: as Minister of Religion and as ambassador to Australia. He has published sixteen books of poetry as well as children's books and two novels. His books have appeared in translation in Albania, Australia, Germany, Italy, Macedonia, Romania, and the United States. The recipient of many literary awards, he lives in Belgrade, where he is currently director of the Ivo Andrić Foundation.

STANISLAVA LAZAREVIĆ was born in Belgrade in 1955. She studied English Language and Literature at Belgrade University, graduating in 1977. Her literary translations into English have been *Death's Homeland* and *Invoking God,* both by Dragan Dragojlović. She also translated into Serbian *The Last Pack of Dingoes,* a book of short stories by Australian author D. Wongar.

Curbstone Press, Inc.
is a non-profit publishing house dedicated to multicultural literature
that reflects a commitment to social awareness and change, with an
emphasis on contemporary writing from Latino, Latin American,
and Vietnamese cultures.

Curbstone's mission focuses on publishing creative writers whose work
promotes human rights and intercultural understanding, and on
bringing these writers and the issues they illuminate into the
community. Curbstone builds bridges between its writers and the
public—from inner-city to rural areas, colleges to cultural centers,
children to adults, with a particular interest in underfunded public
schools. This involves enriching school curricula, reaching out to
underserved audiences by donating books and conducting readings
and educational programs, and promoting discussion in the media.
It is only through these combined efforts that literature can truly
make a difference.

Curbstone Press, like all non-profit presses, relies heavily on the
support of individuals, foundations, and government agencies to bring
you, the reader, works of literary merit and social significance that
would likely not find a place in profit-driven publishing channels, and
to bring these authors and their books into communities across
the country.

If you wish to become a supporter of a specific book—one that is
already published or one that is about to be published—your
contribution will support not only the book's publication but also its
continuation through reprints.

We invite you to support Curbstone's efforts to present the diverse
voices and views that make our culture richer, and to bring these
writers into schools and public places across the country.
Tax-deductible donations can be made to:
Curbstone Press, 321 Jackson Street, Willimantic, CT 06226
phone: (860) 423-5110   fax: (860) 423-9242
www.curbstone.org